The T

D0884784

After fifteen years of futile striving to exact revenge on the Fosdykes after his father's death-bed decision to give the tripeworks to them, Roger Ditchley is still toiling at his life's angry and bitter mission. The blind, insensate hatred driving him on has, over the years, become even more intense, and the fulminating snipe-nosed son of a tripe king will not, cannot, rest while Jos, Rebecca, Tom, Albert, Victoria and Tim Fosdyke occupy the place in the tripe sun which he fervently believes is rightfully his!

The Tripemasters

A Further Helping of the Fosdyke Saga

Bill Tidy

METHUEN

also available from Methuen
Fosdyke Saga: Twelve
Fosdyke Saga: Thirteen

other books by the same author
Fosdyke Saga One to Eleven (Mirror Books)
Tidy's World (Hutchinson)
The Cloggies (Gnome Press)
Tidy Again (Hutchinson)
The Cloggies Dance Again (Hutchinson)
The Great Eric Ackroyd Disaster (Hutchinson)
The Cloggies Are Back (Private Eye)
Mine's a Pint — What's Yours? (Pavilion)
Robbie and The Blobbies (Heinemann)

A Methuen Paperback

First published in Great Britain in 1985
by Methuen London Ltd
11 New Fetter Lane, London EC4P 4EE
Copyright © Bill Tidy Ltd 1985
Made and printed in Great Britain

ISBN 0 413 59960 4

British Library Cataloguing in Publication Data

Tidy, Bill
    The Tripemasters: a further helping
    of the Fosdyke saga.
    I.Title
    741.5'942   PN6737.T5

ISBN 0-413-59960-4

This book is sold subject to the condition
that it shall not, by way of trade or otherwise,
be lent, resold, hired out, or otherwise circulated
without the publisher's prior consent in any form
of binding or cover other than that in which
it is published and without a similar condition
including this condition being imposed
on the subsequent purchaser.

Wild and uncontrollable though Roger's obsessive lust for revenge is, it is more than equalled by the Fosdyke family's compulsive drive to spread the gastronomic gospel of tripe worldwide! Through icy, windswept wastes, and steaming tropical jungles, over jagged peaks, and across arid desertlands, against savage primitive foes or Ditchley's grotesque menagerie of cranks and psychopaths, they march resolutely on!

WHAT IS TRIPE?

Rich in Thoratide, Diomycin 2K and Vitamin W,
Tripe could feed the globe, if only the puzzling,
unaccountable and totally unwarranted aura of mystery
and distaste associated with the world's
greatest natural food could be dispelled!
This then is the noble crusade of Jos
and Rebecca, and, with them at the head,
the Fosdyke family will give their all
to start the white, wet and shaky revolution...
But first they face a deadly threat
on their own doorstep...

The Fosdykes' battle to make a world fit, hungry and safe for tripe has been fought on many outlandish fronts, but none more shrouded in Gothic horror than the stately steam rooms of Salford's exclusive watering hole for local Moguls, the Tripenaeum Club. The vapour-wraithed figures lurking in the doorway are vengeance-crazed Roger Ditchley and his departed father's amazing look-alike, the non-English-speaking Chin Lung. The deception begins…

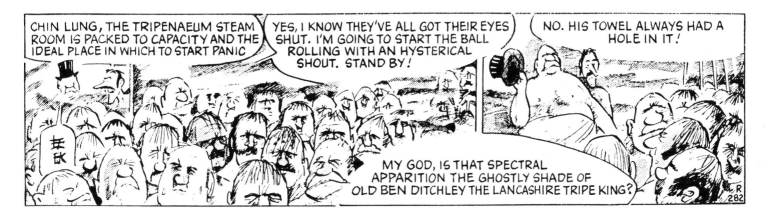

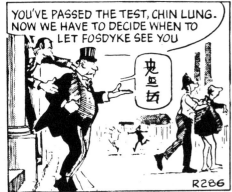

Sir Josiah Fosdyke's wonder horse Tripeworks appears
to have the art world at his hooves, but reckons without the art critics!

Backstage in the Cairo Hippodrome the Amazing Giza has invested Tom Fosdyke with membership of the Inner Ring of the Magic Circle in return for a season at the Salford Slaughterhouse, but will she divulge the secret of invisible tripe?

Fiendishly delighted that Chin Lung can pass off as his long dead father, Roger Ditchley prepares to launch the apparition on the Fosdykes. The first victim he hopes to shock into madness is due to open Pyndrop Hall, home for the Chronically Sharp of Hearing.

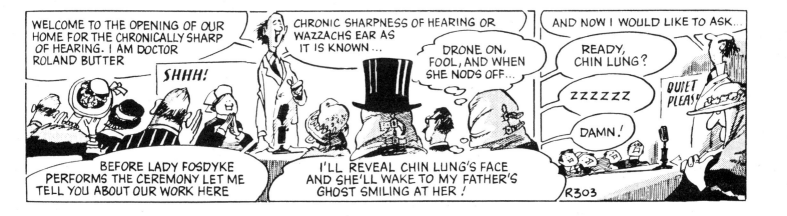

Is it possible that the most despicable of all law officers, a **bent police horse**,
is faking Tripeworks originals? Sir Jos makes enquiries at Truncheon Street Police Station.

In the Egyptian nothingness of the vanished Cairo Hippodrome,
Tom Fosdyke clutches an unseen remnant of invisible tripe.

Lady Fosdyke's piercing scream has shattered the inmates at Pyndrop Hall, home for the Chronically Sharp of Hearing.

Tripehunters' cave, Salford.

Sir Jos Fosdyke (left) indicates the earliest known cave paintings of stone-age tripehunters killing and disembowelling their prey. The tripe was then left to dry in the sun, and eaten later as a type of biscuit or used as a shaving tool. On the right of the picture, Lady Fosdyke covers wall illustrations of a more recent and cruder period.

Where is Rampton the renegade police horse?
Is it really true that he is going at 4½d a slice at Concourt's horsemeat shop?

A world away amidst the shrieking of innumerable parrots,
travel-stained Tom Fosdyke reflects on the events of the last few days.

Adjudicator Victoria Fosdyke moves amongst the delicate matchstick models unaware
that she has been inches away from Ditchley, Chin Lung and disaster.

Not content with forging Tripeworks masterpieces in the secrecy of a dingy garret,
the contemptible Rampton is brazenly accepting commissions on the Queen's Highway in broad daylight!

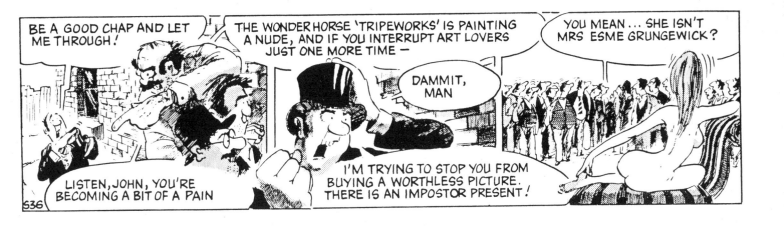

Amanda Pyle-Driver, would-be heavyweight self-sacrifice to Moko the Tripe God,
leads Tom at a cracking pace through the green mansions.

The 'ghost' of Old Ben Ditchley walks! As the vile Ditchley and
his oriental accomplice seek out Tim, a distraught Victoria returns home.

Sir Jos Fosdyke has trailed disgraced ex-police horse 'Rampton'
and his craven rider Nudger Puddington to licensed premises bristling with menace.

The temple of Tripus Maximus, Salford.

All that remains of the once massive structure dedicated to the Roman god of indigestion. Sir Jos stands bare-headed in the ruined Peritoneum, scene of wild, unfettered explosions of feasting and sensuality hailing the celebration of **tripernalia copious**. The next such event takes place on Whit Monday.

A gift to excite and intrigue the simple minds of jungle Indians stands on a hastily cleared jungle lawn. Will it do the trick?

Convinced that they have seen Old Ben Ditchley's ghost, Rebecca and
Victoria Fosdyke turn desperately to vigorous Astral Investigator Tara Clank.

In the notorious 'All Hours' pub, an incredulous Sir Jos Fosdyke
overhears Rampton's gang of miscreants unfold their plans.

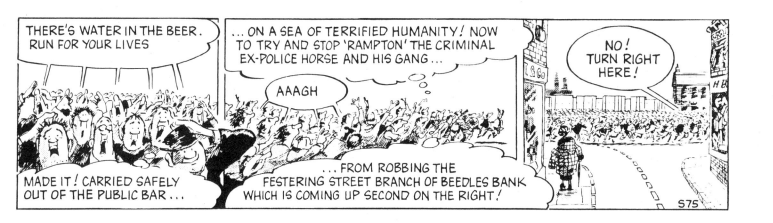

Is it asking too much, even of a woman who catches piranha fish
with her bare hands, to hold back an entire tribe of jungle Indians?

Tara Clank, scourge of the restless male spirit world, seeks out
Ditchley's ghost in the Fosdyke home, where mother and daughter wait nervously.

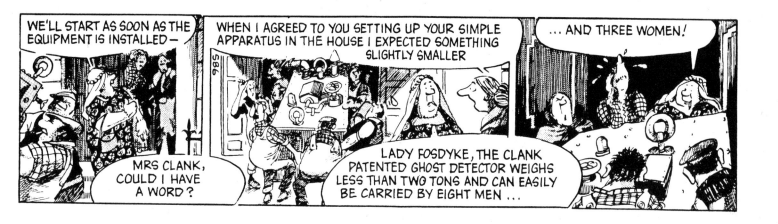

Sir Jos Fosdyke's intimation of the presence of the most dangerous substance
known to drinkers has flushed him out of the 'All Hours' as part of an hysterical human flood.

With the distaff side of the Fosdyke family safely frightened out of their wits,
Roger Ditchley now turns with infinite care to the youngest Fosdyke.

On the peak of a lofty tripe pyramid hidden deep
in the vastness of the Matto Grosso a strange auction takes place…

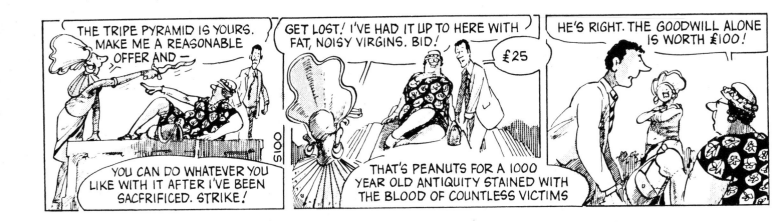

'**Get ye to the devil with yon fenfual fubftance.**'
Cedric Flattley
(Witchfinder General).

Mistress Sedgewyck at the stake.

When Cromwell's Roundheads took Salford after a sharp engagement in 1653 tripe's unfortunate association with 'bundling' and licentious pleasures doomed Mistress Anne 'Busty' Sedgewyck to the pyre. The proprietress of the 'Old Trype Inne' in Salford was secured to the stake, but when the Parliamentarians left forty-three days later the faggots remained unlit. 'Busty' returned to the tap room.

Tara Clank's large device is in position in the Fosdyke residence. All is now ready…

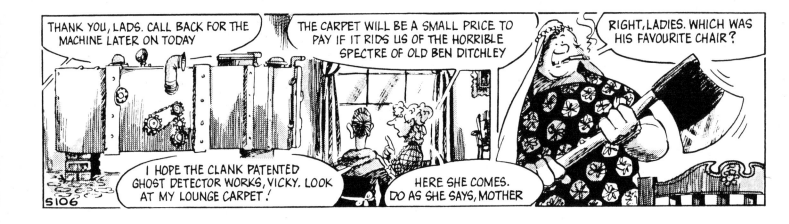

Equine master-criminal Rampton with his intimate knowledge of
Manchester's rooftops has left Sir Jos Fosdyke in an embarrassing position.

Inside McPilloch's gym, Roger Ditchley and Chin Lung seek their third Fosdyke victim.

Across the bloodstained altar of Moko, on the summit of the tripe pyramid, a deal is struck.

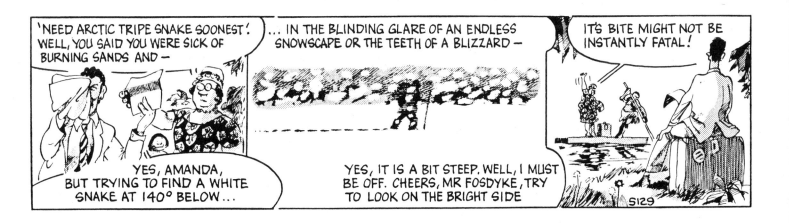

The tree in which Old Ben Ditchley was born and Tara Clank's Patented Ghost Detector apparatus.
Is there a psychic presence in those stark branches?
If there is, the T.C.P.G.D. will flush it out.

A stunned and shocked Sir Jos leaps to the defence of the horse he loves.

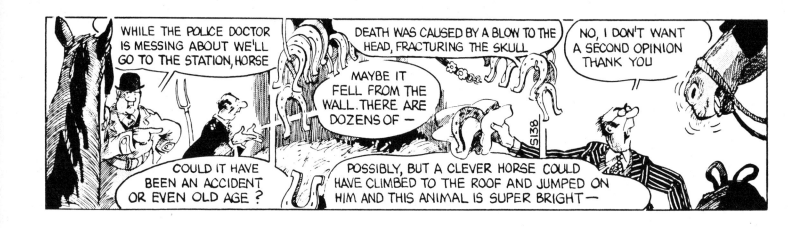

By a strange quirk of fate, Roger Ditchley turns the rope as
ace fitness freak Tim Fosdyke demonstrates his expertise at McPilloch's Gym.

'Had she said
"Let them eat tripe",
there would have been
no French Revolution.'
Robespierre
Paris, 1790.

At sea in Northern latitudes, a perplexed Tom Fosdyke combs the knowledge of
the world's serpentologists to gain some inkling of the magnitude of his next quest...

Who would imagine that in a grimy Salford backyard
one of the rarest miracles of the ornithological world would manifest itself…?

Rampton's gang of cut-throats and footpads have encountered Tripeworks!

An unusually happy and relaxed Roger Ditchley reviews his successful campaign against the hated Fosdykes, and muses on further developments.

The Arctic, scene of Tom Fosdyke's latest and most difficult challenge.

Appearances by Old Ben Ditchley's 'ghost' in assorted sartorial guises
have prompted Lady Fosdyke to seek medical aid for her bed-ridden son, Tim.

The streets of Salford ring to the clash of hoof on cobble as, amidst the showers of sparks,
the noble Tripeworks and his fellow steed and super-crook Rampton fight for good and evil!

Is tripe better than meat?
The great controversy answered at last!

In April 1985 two Olympic medallist weightlifters agreed to take part in a controlled dietary experiment.

Reginald Nutterly (72) ate nothing but fillet steak every day for three months.
Walter Hinchcliffe (141) ate nothing but tripe every day for three months.
On 2 July 1985 Reg and Wally appeared at Salford Health Centre and attempted an individual lift of 270K (400lb).

Reg Nutterly accomplished a clean lift with contemptuous ease. Walter Hinchcliffe could not lift the weights from the mat, and ten minutes later collapsed and died in hospital **but...**

they could not get the lid on his coffin!

A certain sourness has overcome Roger Ditchley's elation, as, mistaken
for Gaelic aerialist Daring O'Duff, he is secured to Albert Fosdyke's aircraft.

At Captain Gladys Blubber's Whaling Station, Tom Fosdyke dines with his gracious hostess.

Reduced to desperation, the Fosdykes clutch at Astral straws...and railway officials.

Frantic to escape lawful retribution and Tripeworks' scything hooves
the despicable Rampton has seized an infant in its pram…

As the wretched Ditchley struggles to free himself from Daring O'Duff's wing-walking harness,
he ponders on the sudden downturn in his fortunes.

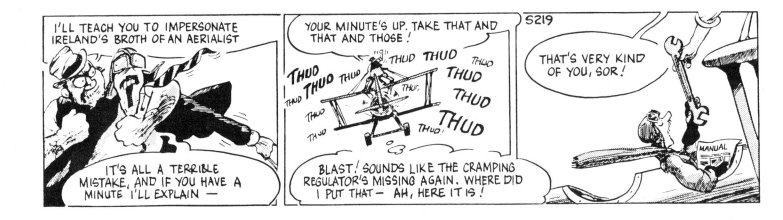

Two lonely figures strike out over the blinding ice mass pushing remorselessly on, each with his own aim in mind.

Amidst the hissing steam and piercing whistles at Salford Central,
a horribly recognisable figure has appeared.

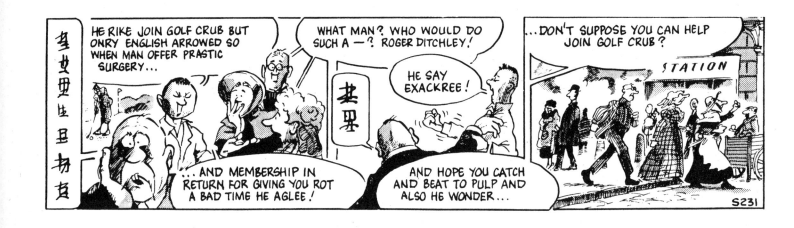

One of the weirdest sea mysteries of all time concerned the tripe schooner **Agnes Gubbins**. Six days out of Bombay she was sighted drifting under bare poles. After signals were ignored a boarding party discovered that her master and crew had left a half-eaten, and still warm meal of tripe vindaloo with Salford dressing and disappeared! After searching the **Agnes**, and sampling the most novel and interesting tripe dish they had ever come across, the boarding party, with plates for their shipmates, returned to the **Marie Celeste**.

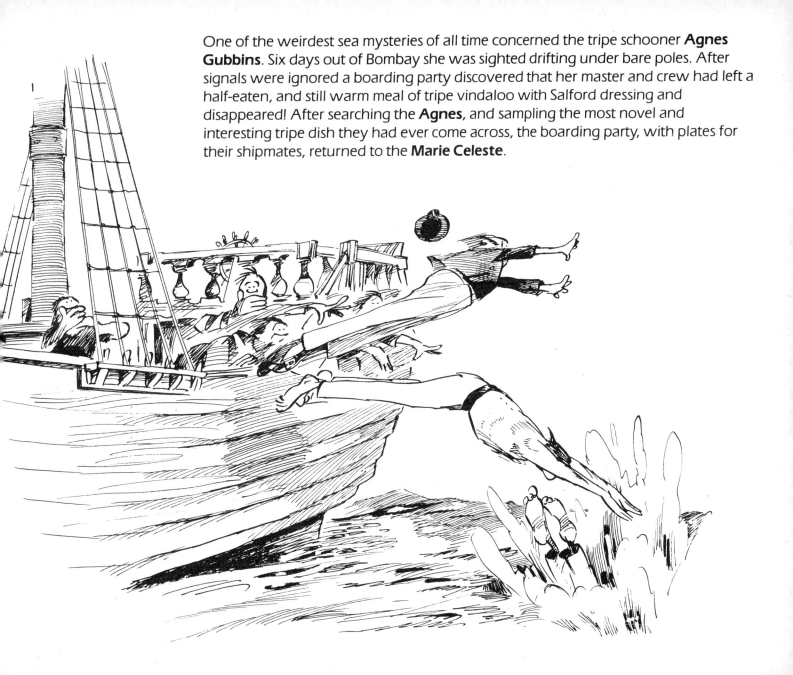

The police marksman's arrow hangs for a moment at the apogee of its flight
and then plummets down, but the unspeakable Rampton has no intention of being struck by it!

High above the streets of Salford, as Albert Fosdyke hurls his flimsy craft about the sky, his passengers state their respective cases.

Abandoned in the cheerless Arctic by his thieving companion Charles,
Tom Fosdyke wonders whether he should go to the scoundrel's aid...

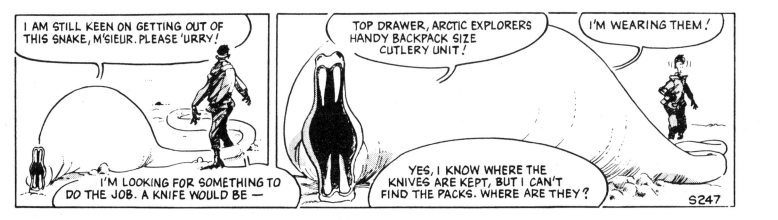

In the Fosdyke home, and in the absence of Sir Jos,
a vitally important meeting takes place.

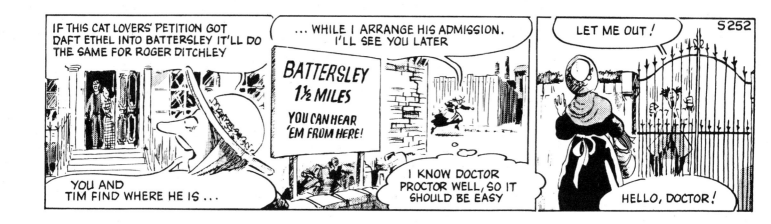

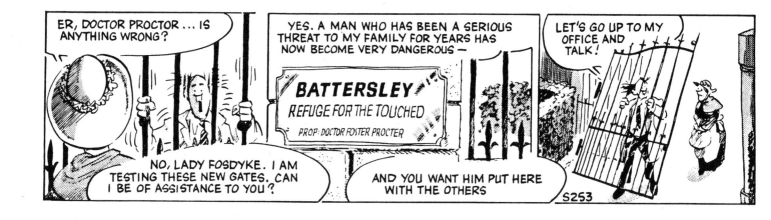

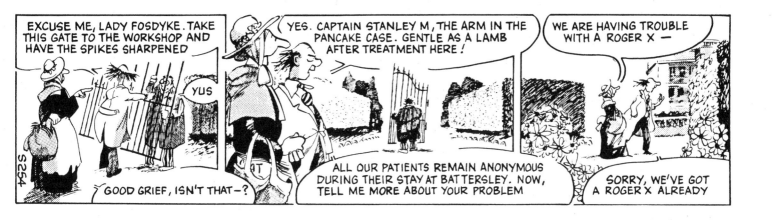

Outside Hacksaw-Johnson ward, a worried Sir Josiah Fosdyke contemplates
the arrow which felled Tripeworks, and thinks of the consequences.

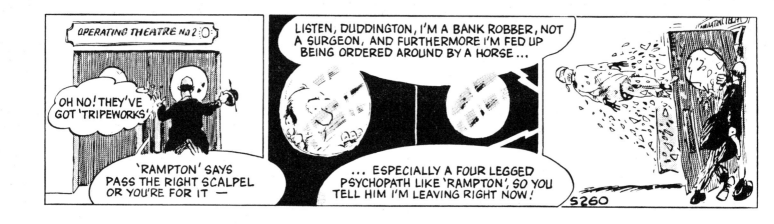

As Albert Fosdyke's wrecked aircraft teeters perilously on the factory chimney hundreds of feet above the ground, his ejected and unwelcome passenger Roger Ditchley gleefully complicates matters from an adjacent structure.

Horrified, Tom sees that his erstwhile betrayer
is now part of the rare white tripe snake.

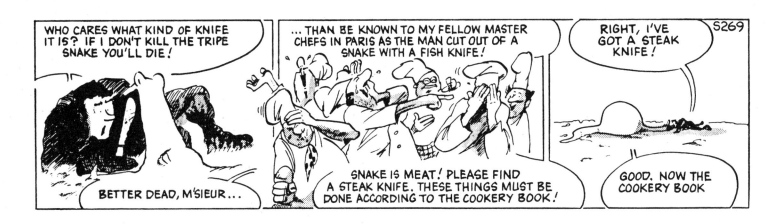

Who can forget Christmas 1916, in France, when after years in the trenches British and German soldiers met in No-Man's Land and exchanged cigarettes, plum and apple jam and family photos? It was later said that the dreadful carnage might well have ended there and then had not Fusilier Albert Pye of the Royal East Salfords not offered Feldwebel Ernst Heidenseeck a plate of Bellingham's best tinned tripe, unaware that Ernst and his chums had been living off nearly 16,000 tons of fresh Fosdyke tripe captured four months earlier!

Can the kindly Lady Fosdyke find a place at Battersley for the maniacal Ditchley?

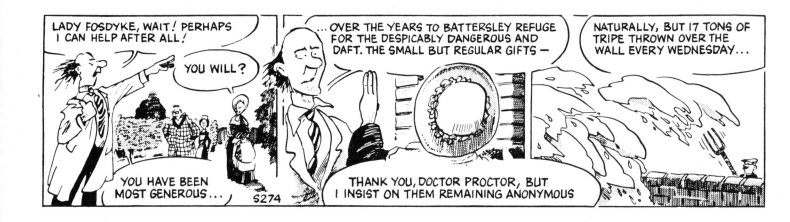

Donning the unconscious thug's surgical garb, Sir Jos enters
the operating theatre in a desperate bid to save his wonder horse.

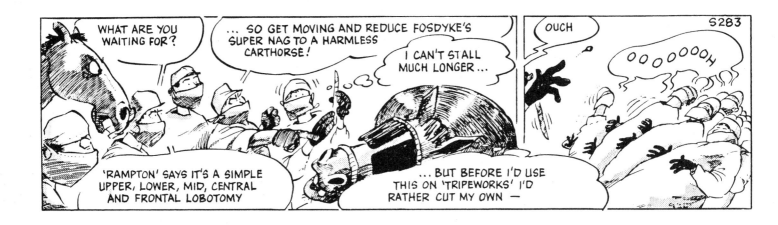

With the muscular Murphy brothers temporarily subdued beneath a hail of bricks, the hate-crazed Ditchley can now devote his entire attention to Albert Fosdyke trapped on the next chimney top.

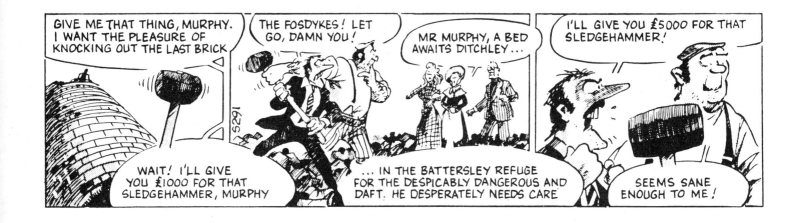

Trapped inside the exotic snow serpent homicidal kitchen king Charles discusses the ingredients of a quiche release.

Ditchley and the Fosdykes face each other
across the piles of fallen bricks, as the bidding rockets!

The most evil equine in the world, disgraced ex-police horse Rampton,
is somewhere in Salford Infirmary. Sir Jos Fosdyke and Tripeworks seek him out.

A repentant Charles unburdens his guilt to Tom Fosdyke as,
with their prize, they near Blubber's Whaling Station.

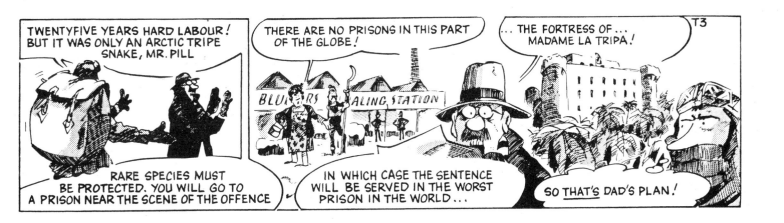

Of all the world's diverse races, colours and religions only one tiny ethnic group, the pitiful remnants of the once mighty Olot tribe, cannot eat tripe! The three surviving members of 41A, The Railings, Salford know that seconds after starting their ritual tripe feast the man downstairs will bang on the ceiling, and complain about the dancing!

Once again fate has intervened and the scheming Roger's plan
to condemn Albert to conjugal servitude with Shamrock Murphy has boomeranged.

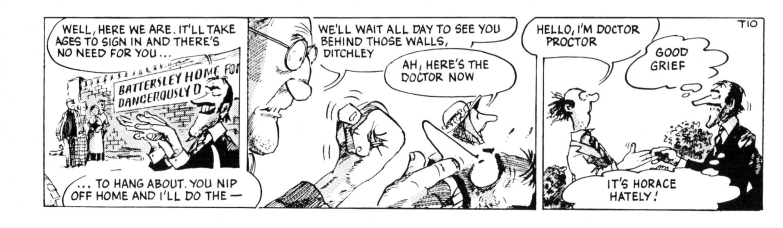

The plan by quadruped criminal mastermind Rampton to
pose as a multiple-broken-leg patient has been exposed.

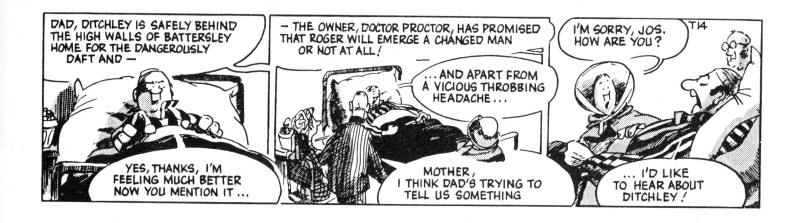

As the **SS Hernia** steams relentlessly on with
her sullen cargo of hopeless prisoners, Tom Fosdyke considers his fate.

Unknown to the Fosdykes, Ditchley's incarceration in Battersley Home
for the Dangerously Daft is not proving to be as beneficial as they had hoped.

While the miscreant nag Rampton appears before
Justice Screecher at Salford Crown Court, Jos Fosdyke muses…

Tom's meeting with Guillotine maintenance man Bernard Flue was an unexpected bonus, but how can he further a passing maritime acquaintanceship?

In the splintered shambles of her room at Battersley Home for the Dangerously Daft, Roger Ditchley comes face to face with his next ally.

The sealed envelopes have been opened and read,
with reactions of horror, amazement and delight.

A horse on trial, an unexpected stage career, a death-defying tripe chute jump,
and the threat of marriage. It is a situation normal for the tripe-missionary Fosdykes,
but what of arch-enemy Roger Ditchley behind the walls of Battersley Home for the Dangerously Daft?

WAIT AND SEE!